ABOVE THE TOP:
A Workable System to Make More Money with Less Management.

By

JOHN K. GLOVER

TABLE OF CONTENTS

CHAPTER ONE

What exactly is a recruiting strategy?

In order to effectively find, attract, and hire the top applicants for your open positions, you need to have a recruiting strategy. These are some fundamental building blocks that can assist you in finding the job applicants you desire. They vary from straightforward techniques, like posting jobs on job boards, to more sophisticated ones, like working with a conventional recruiting firm or developing an employee referral program. At each stage of the hiring process, you can use recruitment tactics.

Finding great talent through recruitment methods

1. Treat applicants as clients

A candidate's initial perception of your business is crucial, whether it be during a phone screening, video interview, or in-person interview. It's crucial to give them the impression that you're as eager to get to know them as they are to be regarded for the position. Treating interviewees the same as your clients is one of the best recruiting strategies.

Show consideration for their time. Always make sure to arrive on schedule, whether it's a phone call, video conference, or in-person meeting. Inform the applicant as soon as you can if you anticipate being late.

Be gracious. Ask if they'd like something to drink and direct them to the restroom when an applicant arrives for an on-site interview. Make them feel at home and welcomed.

Offer to be accessible. Give prospective applicants your contact details so they can get in touch with you with any questions or concerns during the hiring process.

2. Produce enticing work descriptions

One of the most crucial steps in the hiring process is creating a compelling and comprehensive work description.

Here are some ideas to think about:

Titles should be as precise as you can. Your ability to attract the most qualified and enthusiastic job searchers will increase with the accuracy of your title.

Start with an intriguing synopsis. Give a summary that inspires interest in the position and the business among job seekers.

Specify the necessities. Write down the primary duties, hard and soft skills, daily tasks, and an explanation of how the job fits into the company.

3.Utilize social media.

Social media is an excellent instrument for hiring. Social recruiting promotes a two-way dialogue and enables you to share job postings with your complete network. It's possible that the individuals you contact know someone who would be a good fit, even if they aren't interested in the position you're hiring for. Additionally, you can offer prospective employees a glimpse into your company culture by posting images and videos that reflect your employer brand from workplace activities, company events, and/or regular office life.

4. Use supported employment to your advantage.

The visibility of your job ad may wane over time due to Indeed's daily posting of thousands of new jobs. A sponsored job is one of the best ways to guarantee that your job ad remains distinctive. These paid postings are more prominent in any pertinent search results and won't revert to a lower position over time like free job listings, which may attract more qualified applicants. As soon as you pay to post a job, you'll also gain access to Instant Match, which gives you a list of applicants whose resumes match your job requirements on Indeed right away.

5. Establish a scheme for employee referrals

Great individuals frequently surround themselves with other accomplished professionals. Even though many of your workers might already be recommending the best candidates they know for open positions to qualified contacts in their networks, a well-designed employee referral program can motivate even more of them to do so. To generate interest in the program, think about offering bonuses and competitions as referral rewards.

6. Examine internet resumes

Millions of resumes submitted by job seekers from virtually every sector and location are stored on Indeed Resume. By entering a job title or skill along with a city, state or zip, employers can discover candidates fast. Results can be filtered based on factors such as years of expertise, educational attainment, and more. You can also set up a Resume Alert to get daily emails with links to fresh resumes that fit the requirements for the jobs you're trying to fill.

7. Examine previous prospects

When you hire someone for a job, there are frequently a few excellent candidates who don't get the job done because of timing or other outside variables. Consider reviewing the resumes of prior candidates when you're hiring for a job that is similar. These applicants are already acquainted with your business and may have acquired new knowledge and experience since our last conversation.

8. Make your company page your own.
Before applying for jobs, job seekers frequently take the time to study employer reviews, salary information, benefits, and more. You can find all of this information on the Indeed Company Page. Every organization that posts positions on Indeed has a Company Page. You can react to reviews, edit your profile, and add your employer branding by claiming your Company profile.

9. Go to industry-related gatherings

While non-recruiting-specific events are a great way to meet motivated industry professionals eager to network and progress in their field, job fairs can be useful for finding qualified candidates. Find a local organization, meetup, or association that is focused on software development, for instance, and go to a local meeting if you are looking to employ a software engineer. The experts who are most committed will emerge first.

10. Invite your colleagues to the interview.

Sometimes the individual conducting the interview is someone who currently holds the same or a related position. This employee can confirm whether candidates have the qualifications and experience required to perform the work successfully because they already know what it takes to succeed in the role.

Additionally, current workers can accurately describe the working environment and offer prospective employees a better idea of what to anticipate if they are hired.

CHAPTER TWO

RECRUITING MISTAKES

If you avoid a few common pitfalls, you can find the ideal candidate for the position and your company. This article examines 10 hiring errors and suggests ways to prevent them.

10 Common Recruitment Mistakes

There is no surefire method for effective recruitment, but being aware of the challenges and issues you might encounter can help you avoid them or deal with them if they do.

1st Recruitment Error: failing to produce a precise job description

In your advertisement, correctly and honestly describe the position. If you don't, it's less likely that you'll find applicants who have the skills and traits you need.

A good job description goes beyond a straightforward list of responsibilities; it should also outline the role's general goal, highlight major areas of accountability, and list the particular competencies required for success. To avoid misleading applicants into thinking the position provides more opportunities than it actually does, be careful not to "oversell" the position. For instance, if there isn't a chance of a quick promotion, don't suggest that there is. If you do, your eager new hire might feel disappointed and depart.

2nd Recruitment Error: Ignoring Internal Recruiting

The best prospects might occasionally be right in front of you!

Internal hiring can be more cost-effective because it eliminates the need to spend money and effort advertising for outside candidates. Additionally, a current employee will be acquainted with the procedures, principles, and purpose of your company. They probably would acclimate to a new position faster than an outsider would.

Your own employees' morale and efficiency can be raised by promoting and developing them. Additionally, you'll probably gain access to information and expertise from other areas of the company that could improve dialogue and teamwork.

3rd Recruitment Error: Relying too heavily on the interview

Some hiring managers only interview applicants, but is this the most effective approach?

Interviewers may spend the majority of their time attempting to confirm the image they had of candidates after only meeting them for 10 seconds.

Utilizing competency-based interviews is one way to prevent this. To better understand how they might function "on the job," think about adding a test or exercise to these. To find out, for instance, how adept they may be at prioritizing, planning, organizing, and speaking, use the Inbox/In-Tray Assessment.
Diverse methods of skill and behavior assessment will also enable a diverse variety of candidates to stand out. After all, not every member of the squad, no matter how good they may be, can perform at their peak under pressure. This is particularly true if they are, for instance, dyslexic, autistic, or having trouble with an inadequate internet link.

At the least, be sure to invite colleagues from beyond your usual circle to contribute to selection and to constructively challenge your judgment.

4th Recruitment Error: Using unconscious bias

Your ability to make decisions in the recruitment process depends on it, so you must be aware of unconscious bias. You might unintentionally favor applicants who match your background, social class, ethnicity, age, or gender over those who do not.

Accepting applicants despite any of those traits increases your pool of talent from which to choose, increasing your chances of hiring the most qualified candidate.

However, since unconscious prejudice is something you are by definition not aware of, attempting to ignore it will probably not be effective. Create systems that counteract or prevent its impacts instead, like anonymized shortlisting.

5th Recruitment Error: Choosing candidates who are less qualified than you

Some managers are reluctant to hire someone who has greater self-assurance or talent because they worry that they might pose a danger to their position. But astute managers are aware that their teams require intelligent individuals who can contribute their thoughts and strengths.

Hiring superior candidates can help you advance your career and your company.

6th Recruitment Error: rejecting a candidate who is overqualified

It can be tempting to pass over an applicant who is overqualified, either for the same reason as in Mistake 5 above or out of concern that they will get bored and abandon your company in search of a more interesting challenge.

However, highly skilled and talented individuals may have the knowledge and aptitude to aid in the development of your team, even if they don't remain for very long. Consider what opportunities for growth, advancement, or reward you might be able to give to this exceptional person in order to entice them to stay loyal to your company.

7th Recruitment Error: waiting for the ideal applicant

While you wait for the perfect employee to show up, you might be jeopardizing your team's productivity by having it understaffed for an extended period of time. The additional job load or overtime required of your team members may have an impact on their morale.

Because they are so uncommon, recruiters refer to ideal prospects as "purple squirrels"! It's generally best to employ someone who meets the majority of your key requirements, fits your corporate culture, and has good soft skills rather than waiting for someone who perfectly fits the position. Once employed, they can learn the abilities necessary for their position.

8th Recruitment Error: Rushing the Process

Okay, so there might not be a perfect choice. However, that does not imply that you should immediately employ anyone. Give it some time. Consider the time and money it will take to recruit and train someone only to discover they are not qualified for the position. It might be necessary to redo the entire procedure.

If required, conduct two interviews. When you still can't find the best candidate, make arrangements for a contractor from outside the company to fill the position.

9th Recruitment Error: Relying Too Much on References

How much of a resume's content can you believe?

Although applicants might have mentioned excellent experience and qualifications, you should probably verify the accuracy of their claims. Asking for references is one method to achieve this.

Do not, however, give references—whether positive or negative—excessive weight. A person's success at one company does not guarantee that they will succeed at another. Furthermore, just because a former boss gave them a bad review does not guarantee that they won't succeed on your team.

As we mentioned earlier, by assigning a test or exercise that is pertinent to the position that you are advertising, you can determine whether an applicant has the skills necessary for your team. You can take steps in the first few weeks of an appointment with you to identify issues early. Continue reading to learn more.

10th Recruitment Error: expecting too much too soon of a new hire

Don't presume that the appointee will "hit the ground running" because of your careful selection procedure.

A new hire typically needs three months to fully integrate into a team and start making a major impact. It's understandable to want to see an effect more quickly, particularly if the position has been vacant for a while, but this can mean that you don't give them the time to "learn the ropes" properly.

It's crucial to support your new hire as they learn during the first few weeks and assist them in becoming familiar with the organization's and team's objectives. On their first day, welcome them and introduce them to the staff. Inform them that they are welcome to pose questions and seek guidance, and set up regular meetings to check in on them.

There is more to the recruitment plan than simple design. The fundamental recruitment measures to assess the effectiveness of the employment strategy are included in a well-designed recruitment strategy.

It's a good idea to have a backup plan in place in case the backup plan is lost or damaged. The daily improvement method should include the recruitment strategy. The minor upgrades contribute to the development of the competitive edge.

www.ingramcontent.com/pod-product-compliance
Lightning Source LLC
LaVergne TN
LVHW052116160826
845678LV00015B/3589